Super Jobs in Comic Books

Freddie Franco

SCHOLASTIC INC.

New York Toronto London Auckland Sydney
Mexico City New Delhi Hong Kong Buenos Aires

**Cover and opening illustrations
George Toomer**

With special thanks to Trina Robbins.

ISBN 0-439-12384-4
(meets NASTA specifications)

18 17 16 15 14 13 12   23   12 11 10 09

Contents

Introduction

They've got superheroes. They've got cool drawings. They've got battles between good and evil. No wonder comic books attract so many readers. And no wonder so many people dream of creating them.

Two high school buddies in Cleveland, Ohio, created the first comic book. Jerry Siegel and Joe Shuster had an idea for a flying superhero with x-ray vision. They printed their first issues on the school copying machine. Then, in 1938, they published a book about him.

That superhero was the one and only Superman. The book was called Action Comics #1. It was an instant success. More and more comic books followed.

Comic books became very popular. Some were selling a million copies per month! The books were bigger in those days, too. Some were as long as 64 pages. They often included four or five different stories.

It was impossible for one person to turn out

all those pages each month. So an assembly-line system was developed. One person wrote the story. Another person drew it. Someone else inked the drawings. Other artists would do the lettering and the coloring.

This is still the way most comics are produced today. In this book, you'll meet people who work on this "assembly line."

One of the pros in this book is Buzz. He says the team that puts together a comic book is like a group of mad scientists.

"The writer lays out the plans," Buzz explains. "The penciler draws the bones. The inker puts meat on the bones. The colorist adds the skin. And the letterer makes the creature speak."

This is good news for anyone who loves comics. It takes many people to put together one comic book. So there are a lot of opportunities in the industry.

And here's another news flash. These mad scientists love their jobs. The creative people in this book have loved comics since they were little kids.

They were the high school students with lots

of imagination. They were the girls who filled their schoolbooks with doodles. They were the boys who sketched funny pictures of their teachers. They were the kids who made up wild stories for their friends.

They turned their talents into careers in comic books. Keep reading to find out how. But first, brush up on your comic-book vocabulary.

Here are some words and phrases that people who create comic books use all the time.

narration: a phrase or sentence that describes the action of the story

dialogue: words spoken by the characters

panel: a frame or box that contains a scene

speech balloon: the circle in which a character's words are written

storyboard: a series of panels. Comic-book artists use storyboards to plan how a book will look.

thumbnail sketch: a quick, very rough drawing

1 The Man with the Plan
Eddie Berganza, Editor

Who will be the next **villain** to challenge the Man of Steel? Just ask Eddie Berganza. He's the editor of four Superman comic-book series for DC Comics. Berganza decides who Superman will fight each week.

The editor's job is to oversee the process of creating a comic book. Berganza's in charge of everything from the idea for the story to the details of the art.

"The first thing I do," Berganza says, "is hire the writer. The writer comes up with an idea for an issue—or several issues."

Berganza then works with the writer. He makes sure the story idea doesn't **contradict** past stories about Superman. Berganza edits four different Superman titles. So he has to keep his facts straight. He uses detailed charts to track the action over the past few years. After reviewing the charts, Eddie may suggest changes to make the story fit the character's history.

Fortunately, in the comic-book world, you can bend the rules of reality. "That's one of the cool things about comic books. No character really dies and stays dead," Berganza says.

"A character might be killed. And we might swear he's dead, dead, dead. But another editor can come along and **resurrect** him," he says. "It's just a matter of being creative about bringing him back." Berganza has even brought Superman himself back from the dead.

After working on the script, Eddie's next step is hiring the right penciler. That's the artist who sketches the book's pages. "I try to find a penciler who will bring out the best in the writer's work,"

YOUNG JUSTICE #34: pencils by Todd Nauck: Inks by Lary Stucker

Super Eddie: Berganza was once cast as a superhero in one of DC's comic books!

Eddie checks out the latest issue of *Superman* in his New York City office. Copies of inked pages for future issues about the Man of Steel hang on the bulletin board behind him.

Berganza explains.

Berganza then hires an inker, who traces the penciled lines with ink and adds shading and details. Next, he chooses a colorist, who colors the inked drawings. And he picks a letterer to place the characters' dialogue in the artwork. (For more information about these jobs, see Chapters 2, 3, 4, 5, and 6.)

Berganza's goal is to hire artists whose styles work well together. It makes for a better book.

And it keeps the artists happy. "Say the artists aren't pleased with each other's work. Then the editor's job becomes very difficult!" Eddie says.

Each book takes months of hard work. Along the way, Berganza has to make sure everyone gets their work done on time. "Everyone works against the clock, " Berganza says. "Editors spend hours asking people to turn their work in on time."

After the artwork and lettering are finished, Berganza reviews the pages. Then, the cover and advertisements are added. Finally, the comic book is printed and shipped to stores.

This job is a dream come true for Berganza. "I was a fan of comic books from early on," he says. "I loved them. I would spend all my allowance on comics."

Today, Berganza's office walls and shelves are covered with comic-book posters and toys. He also gets tons of free comic books to read. "It's a great perk of the job," Eddie says.

Berganza got his big break in the business years ago. He found out about a job in the mailroom at DC Comics. He jumped at the opportunity. Then he worked his way up from there. (That's a long way up, in case you're wondering.)

Now Berganza's at the top. And he gets a lot of satisfaction from his job. "I want to inspire the artists and writers who work with me to do their best," Berganza says. "And, of course," he adds, "I want to make sure that Superman keeps winning those battles against the forces of evil!"

2 Fighting Words
Mark Waid, Writer

Mark Waid likes to start trouble. His words start some of the worst fights in the world. The world of comic books, that is.

As a comic-book writer, Waid has created battles for many characters, including The Flash, Captain America, and Batman, just to name a few. Now, he is senior writer for CrossGen Comics. There, he writes stories for *Ruse,* a detective series, and *Negation,* a science fiction series.

But Waid's work is not all about big explosions and hand-to-hand combat. For him, writing has a greater purpose. "As a writer, your job is to show people something they've never seen before," he says. "I try to challenge people. I want to make them look at the world in a different way."

Most of Mark's stories begin with a simple idea. Sometimes it's his own idea. Sometimes the idea comes from his editor. Then, to get started, Waid asks himself questions about his characters. "Who are their enemies? What can harm them? What is something they have never done? What do I like about them?"

Maureen McTigue

Editors and writers often call Mark Waid to tap his knowledge of comic-book history and trivia.

Next, Waid develops a **plot**. That's the story. What happens first? Next? Last? Which villain will cause trouble this time? And how will the superhero stop the evil plan? Waid talks again with the editor. Then it's time to write the script.

A comic-book script includes art directions, narration, and dialogue. The art directions give the artist ideas about how the panel should look. The narration often describes where and when the action in the panel is taking place.

The dialogue is what the characters say to

each other. Dialogue can also be sound effects—you know, like *Blam!* or *Kerpow!* (For an example of a script, see "Picture This" on page 19.)

What's the secret to a great script? For Waid, it's drawing on personal experience. "No one really knows how it feels to fly," he says. "But we all know how it feels when the final bell rings on the last day of school. That must be how Superman feels when he takes off into the air."

Once his script is complete, Waid turns it over to the artist. He's often amazed and surprised by the artists' work. "You can never forget that making comic books is a **collaboration**," he says. "A lot of times I'm blown away. Some of these artists are so talented. It's like a dream when it all comes together."

In fact, Waid's whole career has been "like a dream." He's wanted to work in this field since he was a young boy.

He remembers the first comic book he ever bought—at age four. "It was Batman and Robin battling Deathman. Deathman was just a guy in a skeleton costume. It was a goofy story. But I didn't care."

Throughout his adult life, Waid has kept his hands in the comic-book business. He began his career as a reporter, writing about the industry. Then, he became a comic-book editor.

Next, he decided to try writing comic books himself. Over the years, he has written books for every major comic-book company. He's created many of his own heroes and villains.

Waid is also considered an expert in the history of comic books. Every day he gets calls from other writers and editors. "What's the date on the giant penny in Batman's cave?" they'll ask. (It's 1947.) "How about the names of Superman's girlfriend's parents?" (Lois Lane's folks are Sam and Ella.)

Waid's knowledge does have its limits, though. "I may know a lot about comic books," he jokes. "But I can only name 38 states."

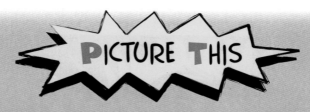

PICTURE THIS

Here's a page from a comic-book script. It's about Odysseus, sort of a Greek superhero. In this panel, Odysseus and his men are trapped in the cave of a cyclops. That's a huge, one-eyed giant.

As you can see, comic-book writers don't just create the character's dialogue. They also give the artists ideas about how each panel should look.

PANEL ONE

[art instructions: The cyclops has grabbed two of Odysseus's men. He holds one struggling man in his huge fist. He stuffs another into his mouth. The other men are in the back of the cave, shaking with fear.]

NARRATION: Meanwhile, back in the cyclops's cave . . .

MAN BEING EATEN: AIEEE!

MAN IN FIST: No, no! Let me go!

CYCLOPS: Humans! My favorite food!

ODYSSEUS: [thought balloon] He'll eat us all unless I do something!

3 Sketchy Character

J.G. Jones, Penciler

J. G. Jones is a penciler. He may have the most desired job in the comic-book industry. You'd think they could come up with a better name for it!

Pencilers are the ones who draw the characters and the action. They bring the story to life.

J.G. Jones has been a penciler for about 10 years. His job is to tell a story with action-packed drawings. He draws battle scenes that seem to burst off the page.

So where does Jones begin? First, he talks about the story with the writer and editor. He then reads over the script. He starts to imagine how things should look. "I try to set up each scene like a film shot," he says.

Jones then makes rough sketches of the

storyboards. As he does, he keeps certain rules in mind. The character who speaks first in a panel is usually drawn on the left side. This makes it easier for the reader to follow what's going on.

J.G. Jones

A self-portrait by J.G. Jones.

Jones must also remember to leave space for the word balloons, where the dialogue is printed.

Next, Jones shows his rough storyboards to the writer and editor and asks for suggestions. Sometimes he has to create several **drafts** before the story and art work together.

Still, Jones has to work fast. "I'm always working against a deadline. That's the only downside to this job," he says, sketching as he speaks. He hands in pages as he finishes them. That way, the other artists can work on the first pages of the book while Jones is still drawing the ending!

Luckily, when Jones sees the finished book, it seems worth it. "I like having a beautiful finished product with my name on it," he says.

Jones has loved comic books since he was little. As a child, he was a fan of Spider-Man and the Fantastic Four. But it wasn't just the superheroes he admired. "Early comic-book artists were my heroes," says Jones.

J.G. Jones

Jones takes a rare break from the drawing table.

He began drawing superheroes as soon as he could hold a pencil. In college, he studied painting. But he always kept his friends laughing by drawing cartoons about their lives.

After graduate school, Jones drew political cartoons for a New York City newspaper. This gave him the courage to follow his childhood dream. He wrote and illustrated his own comic book. It was about a modern vampire.

Soon, Jones got a job with one of the most famous publishers in the comic-book business. Today, he draws famous characters, including Spider-Man and Wonder Woman.

Maybe there's someone right now reading a comic book and saying, "I can't believe what this guy can do." And maybe she's not talking about the superhero who can leap over skyscrapers. Maybe she's talking about J.G. Jones, the artist who makes that superhero leap right off the page.

4 Battle Lines
Buzz, Inker

His name is Buzz. Just Buzz. He's so well known in the comic-book industry that he only needs to use his first name! Buzz is an inker. And he's one of the best in the business.

Using permanent ink, Buzz adds detail and depth to the penciler's sketches. He doesn't just trace the penciler's lines with ink. He makes decisions about the thickness of the lines. He also adds shadows, background details, and fills (the dark parts).

This is difficult work because there is little room for error. Buzz has to be very careful when he's working. A careless mistake can ruin hours of work! "We're not supposed to make mistakes. At least not big ones," Buzz jokes.

One key to avoiding big errors is talking with the penciler. Imagine discovering that it's

supposed to be noon outside instead of midnight. And you've already inked the sky black! "You want to be sure about things like that before you throw ink at it!" warns Buzz.

For fixing small errors, though, Buzz uses special white paint. "And, to be honest, inkers use more than they admit!"

Inkers use a variety of tools. Buzz uses small brushes for curves. He uses drafting pens for straight lines. The pens also come in handy for special effects, like explosions and speed lines. Sometimes, he even dips an old toothbrush in ink to achieve special **textures**, such as star fields.

As he works, Buzz tries to keep in mind the penciler's **intentions**. His goal, he says, is to "bring a flair to the work without changing the original feel and style."

How does someone get interested in inking? For Buzz, the road to becoming an inker started a long time ago.

He was just 13 years old when he moved to the United States from Burma. (Burma is now known as Myanmar.) He couldn't speak

Buzz races against the clock in this caricature of himself.

English when he arrived at his new home in Brooklyn, New York. But he had his own way of communicating with others—art!

Buzz soon learned that drawing helped him make new friends. It also helped him avoid fights. "I drew a picture of Batman for one of the bullies at school. He didn't pick on me after that," he says.

When Buzz was just 17 years old, he got a

big break. He showed his work to an editor at DC Comics. The editor loved his work. He offered Buzz a job on the spot! Buzz began penciling a book called *Dragonlance.* Soon, he was drawing and inking other books, including *X-Men* and *Vampirella.*

But then, Buzz had some bad luck. He injured his drawing hand. There were certain types of pencil and brush strokes he could no longer do.

It could have ended his career. But Buzz taught himself a new way of using the pencils and brushes. He kept inking. And more editors than ever are calling for Buzz—just Buzz.

5 **Bold Type**
Lois Buhalis, Letterer

It's said that a picture is worth a thousand words. But without words, most comic books wouldn't get very far. Comic-book letterers get the words onto the page. And they get them into the mouths of the characters.

Lois Buhalis has been making comic-book characters speak for about 20 years.

After the artists have finished the panels, Buhalis inserts speech balloons, thought balloons, and narration boxes. Then, she adds the words to them. Another part of her job is adding sounds effects. You know, like *Kerpow!* and *BRRUZZT!*

How does she do it? When Lois letters by hand, she first draws light lines to write on. Then she inks in the words with a pen and black ink.

What if the artists didn't leave enough room for the words? It's up to Lois to *find* enough space. "One editor called me the goddess of lettering," she laughs. "I can fit a lot of words into crowded panels."

Buhalis also prides herself on adding a personal touch to the books she works on. "There's a lot more creativity involved in lettering than most people think," she says. She got really wacky when lettering a comic book called *The Mask*. She used several different typefaces and styles. And she added spirals and designs called dingbats.

Trina Robbins

The mysterious Lois Buhalis refuses to be photographed. But she allowed a friend to draw this caricature of her.

These days, Buhalis does most of her work on the computer. She chooses the typeface for dialogue, then pastes the text into the speech balloons. "Computers make it easy to move words and sound effects around," Buhalis says. "And corrections are easier. There's no sitting around, waiting for that white-out to dry!"

Still, Buhalis recommends learning to letter the old-fashioned way. "It really helps to learn by hand before you try it on the computer," she says.

Buhalis has loved working with letters since she was ten years old. That's when she learned about **calligraphy**. That's the art of writing in fancy scripts. Her mother had taken a course in calligraphy. Lois used her mom's books and supplies. And she managed to teach herself this skill.

Later, Lois decided to combine her love of lettering with her love of comics. She showed her lettering samples to an award-winning letterer. She became his assistant. He had her start with the basics. Her first job was to draw lines with a ruler for him to write on!

Eventually, Buhalis became good enough to work on her own. Since then, she has lettered many different titles, including *The Green*

Lantern, *Spider-Man Annual*, *The New Mutants*, and *Superman Adventures*.

You have to love working with letters to do what Buhalis does. That's because you won't get famous doing it. The attention tends to go to the artists.

"Remember that the art is the most important element," says Buhalis. "Your lettering is there to **mesh** with the art and advance the story. The good news is, as long as there are comic books, they'll be looking for letterers."

6 True Colors
Tom Chu, Colorist

Just a few years back, if you asked a comic-book colorist to get to work, he or she would reach for ink, watercolors, brushes, and pens.

But these days, a colorist is more likely to turn on the computer.

Just ask Tom Chu. He uses his computer to transform inked drawings into full-color images. As far as he's concerned, there's no need to color with inks and watercolors anymore.

"Computers now are fast enough and smart enough to reproduce **traditional** effects," he says. "For example, filters in the computer program can give a brushstroke effect."

In fact, Chu may never actually *touch* the art for a comic book. Often, editors send him

electronic **scans** of pages that have been penciled and inked. He then opens the scan in his software program and gets to work.

For the most part, Chu gets to choose the colors that he thinks will work best. "Usually the editors are pretty flexible," says Chu. But not always. "Sometimes the more established characters require certain colors," Chu explains. Spider-Man's mask is always the same red, for example.

Chu has been using the computer to color comics for several years. He had planned to study comic-book art after high school. But one colorist convinced him that all he needed was the right type of computer. Then he could start learning immediately.

So Chu took a big risk. He sold the computer he owned. And he **invested** the money in the computer the colorist had suggested. He called his new **mentor** and said, "Okay. I got the computer. Now what?"

He then worked with his mentor for three months, learning how to use the software. Soon, he was hired by Crusade Comics. After another year of knocking on editors' doors, he began getting work from the larger companies, including Marvel Comics.

Chu's interest in comic books began when his family moved to the United States from Taiwan. "I got into comics right away," he says. "I liked the heroes and the fantasy stories. Plus, comic books were a great way to start reading English."

Courtesy Tom Chu

Chu tells other young artists to follow their dreams. "Give your talents a chance," he says. "Or you'll never know what you can do."

At first, Chu practiced by tracing figures. Soon, he could draw figures on his own. By the time he got to high school, he'd decided he wanted to work in comics. "Like a lot of typical Asian kids, I helped my family in our restaurant after school," says Chu. "But I didn't make that my **destiny**. I had already chosen another road."

But Chu is not running from his **heritage**.

In fact, he feels that his background gives him a creative advantage.

Chu's caricature of himself.

Tom Chu

"I think that being an immigrant gives me more ideas," Chu says. "I constantly have two cultures in my head. And some of my own comic-book characters are based on my experiences. My background plays a big part in who I am."

George Tuckwell © Scholastic Inc.

Take Cover
Amanda Conner, Cover Artist

Can you judge a book by its cover? Maybe not. But when it comes to selling a comic book, the cover may be the thing that sparks a customer's interest. That's why editors only hire their best artists to draw covers.

And Amanda Conner is one of the best.

Conner's work begins when an editor calls her with an assignment. Conner and the editor talk about the story. Then Amanda comes up with some ideas for the cover. She faxes the editor some rough sketches. The editor picks an idea. And Conner is off.

Conner then pencils a small, finished drawing. Next, she enlarges it to full size and puts it on a light table. That's a thick piece of glass with a light beneath it. She traces the drawing onto heavy paper and creates a final drawing. "I aim for a real eye-catching effect

Amanda lives and works in New York City. That's where many of the comic-book companies she draws for are based.

with my covers," Conner says.

Comics caught *her* eye when she was just a little kid. Whenever she got sick, her mother would buy her the new Archie and Wonder Woman comics. "That was the one good thing about being sick!" she says.

When she was in school, Conner filled her notebook with drawings. Her dream was to draw comics.

After high school, Conner went to art school. Then, she worked in a comic-book store. And then, Conner got a chance to work as a comic-book artist's assistant.

Soon, she was ready to do her own work. In the late 1980s, she started penciling *Wasp* and *She-Hulk* for Marvel Comics. Finally, in 1991, she started drawing covers.

Since then, she's made her mark on the comics scene. Among the many comics she's drawn are *Lois Lane, The Joker, Harley Quinn,* and *Vampirella.*

That's a lot of work, but Conner enjoys it. "Drawing comics is a labor of love," she says. "It should be fun because you won't become a millionaire doing it."

Amanda Conner

Conner's caricature of herself.

"That's what's most important in any career," Conner adds, "doing something that you really love."

8 Combat Zone

Kathy Bottarini, Store Owner

Flash back 20 years ago. If you walked into any drugstore or newspaper shop, you'd see a revolving rack of comic books for sale. These "spinner racks" were everywhere.

Okay, back to the present. The spinner racks are gone. These days, comic books are mostly just sold in stores that **specialize** in comic books.

That's what makes people like Kathy Bottarini key players in the comic-book world. Bottarini owns the Comic Book Box in Petaluma, California. She keeps kids and adults supplied with comics.

Bottarini has loved comics since she was a kid. In fact, her mom used comics to bribe her to go to the dentist. "If we behaved for the dentist," says Kathy, "we'd get comics afterward."

Later, when Bottarini was in college, she got a part-time job working at the Comic Book Box. A few years later, the owner retired and put the store up for sale. "I loved the store, and I decided to make a commitment," Bottarini says. So, she took the plunge and bought the store.

Ever since, Bottarini has worked hard to get new readers. She moved her store next door to a bookstore, and soon the Comic Book Box was attracting new customers. "We have very good

Mary Gow © Scholastic Inc.

Bottarini knows her comic books. And she knows her customers. So she can always suggest what a customer should read next.

traffic between the stores," Bottarini brags.

Bottarini also passes out free comic books at special events in the community. "A lot of kids tell me that it's the first comic book they've ever had," she says. "I always find that surprising."

Bottarini always tries to order books that readers will love. These decisions are **crucial**—because Bottarini loses money on books that don't sell.

So how does she do it? Well, after the store closes, Bottarini catches up on her comic-book reading. (Believe it or not, she's too busy to read during the day.)

She decides what she thinks will be popular. She places her orders. And then she crosses her fingers and hopes that she's right. As Bottarini says, "Catching up on comics is my homework, and placing the orders is my exam."

Fortunately, it's homework Bottarini enjoys. And it's an exam she usually passes with flying colors.

9 **Super Mentor**
Michael Davis, Entrepreneur

A love of comic books and a caring mentor helped Michael Davis become a success in the world of entertainment. Among other things, he is the creative mind behind *Cousin Skeeter,* a TV show on Nickelodeon.

When Davis was young, drawing kept him out of trouble. As he grew older, his mother started to worry that he was on his own too much. So, she arranged for him to start working in his cousin's art studio.

Fortunately for Davis, his cousin was a successful painter, William T. Williams. And Williams took the role of mentor very seriously. He had a favorite saying: "Each one, teach one." He felt that every successful person should take someone under his or her wing.

Williams taught Davis the art of painting

James A. Steinfeldt

For several years, Michael directed the Children's Art Carnival at New York City's Museum of Modern Art. Many future comic-book artists polished their skills under Michael's guidance there.

and helped **launch** Michael's career as a **graphic artist**.

Davis loved comic books, but he did not see working on them as a good career choice. "Actually," he jokes, "they seemed like a sure way to starve and die."

But then Davis changed his mind. He realized that if he owned the rights to the characters and ideas he created, he could make a lot of money. This thinking led Michael and several of this friends to create Milestone Media.

Milestone focused on creating an entire universe of multicultural heroes and villains. It became the most successful African-American-owned comic-book company in the world.

Eventually, Milestone signed a deal to produce cartoons. That's when *Static Shock* hit TV. According to Michael, the character Static, an African-American teenage superhero, is based on his own teenage experiences.

Next, Davis left Milestone to become president of Motown Animation. There, he worked on shows for Disney, ABC, WB, FOX, and Nickelodeon. One of those shows was the incredibly popular *Cousin Skeeter.*

With his great success, Davis has not forgotten his mentor's motto: "Each one, teach one." So, like his own mentor, Davis works with young artists. He encourages them to think of art as a sport.

"Competition is important in this business," says Davis.

Michael Davis

Michael painted several comic books early in his career. Here, he has painted himself as a masked superhero.

He adds, "Seek out the best. Pick the brains of people who are better than you are. Try to learn all you can from them. Then once you've got it, throw some of your own unique moves back at them."

Davis must know what he's talking about. Many of his former students are now professional comic book and animation artists. And Michael's unique moves have lifted him to the top of his field.

A WORK IN PROGRESS

BY THE TIME YOU GET YOUR HANDS ON THE LATEST COMIC BOOK, IT'S GONE THROUGH A LOT OF OTHER PEOPLE'S HANDS. MOST COMIC-BOOK ART IS THE PRODUCT OF SEVERAL DIFFERENT ARTISTS.

TO SHOW YOU THE STAGES OF THAT PROCESS, SEVERAL ARTISTS IN THIS BOOK WORKED TOGETHER TO CREATE A PANEL FOR A SUPERHERO COMIC. HERE ARE THE STEPS ALONG THE WAY.

J.G. Jones

PENCILER *J.G. JONES* CAME UP WITH AN IDEA FOR A SUPERHERO. THEN HE MADE A ROUGH SKETCH. WITH JUST A FEW STROKES OF HIS PENCIL, JONES GAVE THE SUPERHERO AN AGGRESSIVE, IN-YOUR-FACE ATTITUDE.

JONES THEN CREATED A DETAILED DRAWING. YOU GET A MUCH CLEARER VIEW OF THE SUPERHERO. YOU CAN ALSO SEE THAT AN ALIEN ROBOT IS CHASING HIM. NOTICE TWO MORE DETAILS: IN THE BACKGROUND, THOSE SMALL "X'S" SHOW THE INKER WHERE TO COLOR AREAS SOLID BLACK. AND OVER TO THE LEFT, JONES HAS ADDED HIS SIGNATURE.

J.G. Jones

NEXT, INKER BUZZ TOOK JONES'S PENCILED PAGE AND
INKED OVER IT, USING BRUSHES AND PENS. BUZZ'S
DARK SHADOWS ADD DEPTH TO THE DRAWING. THEY
MAKE THE HERO'S FACE AND MUSCLES MORE DEFINED,
TOO. NOTICE THAT BUZZ PLACED HIS OWN SIGNATURE
BELOW JONES'S.

J.G. Jones; Buzz

COLORIST TOM CHU SCANNED THE INKED PAGE INTO HIS COMPUTER. THEN HE COLORED IT, USING AN ART PROGRAM. NOTICE HOW CHU'S COLORING BROUGHT OUT SMALL DETAILS ON THE SUPERHERO'S UNIFORM. SUDDENLY, THERE SEEMS TO BE ELECTRICITY RUNNING THROUGH IT. THEN CHU ADDED HIS SIGNATURE.

J.G. Jones; Buzz; Tom Chu